50 Biscuit and Bread Dishes

By: Kelly Johnson

Table of Contents

- Buttermilk Biscuits
- Cheddar Bay Biscuits
- Southern Drop Biscuits
- Honey Butter Biscuits
- Angel Biscuits
- Garlic Herb Biscuits
- Sweet Potato Biscuits
- Pumpkin Spice Biscuits
- Jalapeño Cheddar Biscuits
- Blueberry Biscuits with Lemon Glaze
- Whole Wheat Biscuits
- Cornmeal Biscuits
- Cream Cheese Biscuits
- Chocolate Chip Biscuits
- Maple Pecan Biscuits
- Cinnamon Sugar Biscuits
- Herb and Parmesan Biscuits
- Red Lobster-Style Biscuits
- Bacon and Cheddar Biscuits
- Greek Yogurt Biscuits
- Buttermilk Drop Biscuits
- Flaky Layered Biscuits
- Cranberry Orange Biscuits
- Almond Flour Biscuits
- Sourdough Biscuits
- Classic French Baguette
- Sourdough Bread
- Ciabatta Bread
- Focaccia with Rosemary and Sea Salt
- Brioche Loaf
- Challah Bread
- Garlic Knots
- Italian Herb and Cheese Bread
- Pita Bread
- Naan Bread

- Cornbread Muffins
- Honey Oat Bread
- Rye Bread
- French Toast Bread
- Cinnamon Swirl Bread
- Banana Bread
- Zucchini Bread
- Pumpkin Bread
- Cranberry Walnut Bread
- Cheddar Jalapeño Bread
- Pretzel Bread Rolls
- Olive and Herb Focaccia
- Potato Bread
- Multigrain Seeded Bread
- Beer Bread

Buttermilk Biscuits

Ingredients:

- 2 cups all-purpose flour
- 1 tablespoon baking powder
- ½ teaspoon baking soda
- 1 teaspoon salt
- ½ cup unsalted butter, cold and cubed
- ¾ cup buttermilk

Instructions:

1. Preheat oven to 425°F.
2. In a bowl, whisk flour, baking powder, baking soda, and salt.
3. Cut in butter until mixture resembles coarse crumbs.
4. Stir in buttermilk until just combined.
5. Roll out dough to ½-inch thickness and cut into rounds.
6. Place on a baking sheet and bake for 12-15 minutes.

Cheddar Bay Biscuits

Ingredients:

- 2 cups all-purpose flour
- 1 tablespoon baking powder
- ½ teaspoon salt
- ½ teaspoon garlic powder
- ½ cup unsalted butter, melted
- 1 cup shredded cheddar cheese
- ¾ cup buttermilk
- 1 tablespoon fresh parsley, chopped

Instructions:

1. Preheat oven to 450°F.
2. Mix flour, baking powder, salt, and garlic powder.
3. Stir in cheddar cheese and buttermilk.
4. Drop dough onto a baking sheet and bake for 10-12 minutes.
5. Brush with melted butter and parsley.

Southern Drop Biscuits

Ingredients:

- 2 cups all-purpose flour
- 1 tablespoon baking powder
- ½ teaspoon salt
- ½ cup cold butter, cubed
- ¾ cup milk

Instructions:

1. Preheat oven to 425°F.
2. Mix flour, baking powder, and salt.
3. Cut in butter until crumbly, then stir in milk.
4. Drop spoonfuls of dough onto a baking sheet.
5. Bake for 12-14 minutes.

Honey Butter Biscuits

Ingredients:

- 2 cups all-purpose flour
- 1 tablespoon baking powder
- ½ teaspoon salt
- ½ cup unsalted butter, cubed
- ¾ cup buttermilk
- 2 tablespoons honey

Instructions:

1. Preheat oven to 425°F.
2. Mix flour, baking powder, and salt.
3. Cut in butter and stir in buttermilk and honey.
4. Roll out and cut into biscuits.
5. Bake for 12-15 minutes.

Angel Biscuits

Ingredients:

- 2 cups all-purpose flour
- 1 tablespoon sugar
- 1 teaspoon baking powder
- ½ teaspoon baking soda
- 1 teaspoon salt
- ½ teaspoon dry yeast
- ½ cup unsalted butter, cubed
- ¾ cup buttermilk

Instructions:

1. Preheat oven to 400°F.
2. Mix flour, sugar, baking powder, baking soda, salt, and yeast.
3. Cut in butter and stir in buttermilk.
4. Let dough rest for 15 minutes.
5. Roll out and cut into biscuits.
6. Bake for 12-15 minutes.

Garlic Herb Biscuits

Ingredients:

- 2 cups all-purpose flour
- 1 tablespoon baking powder
- ½ teaspoon salt
- ½ teaspoon garlic powder
- ½ cup cold butter, cubed
- ¾ cup buttermilk
- 1 tablespoon fresh herbs (parsley, thyme, rosemary), chopped

Instructions:

1. Preheat oven to 425°F.
2. Mix flour, baking powder, salt, and garlic powder.
3. Cut in butter, then stir in buttermilk and herbs.
4. Roll out and cut into biscuits.
5. Bake for 12-15 minutes.

Sweet Potato Biscuits

Ingredients:

- 2 cups all-purpose flour
- 1 tablespoon baking powder
- ½ teaspoon salt
- ½ teaspoon cinnamon
- ½ cup unsalted butter, cubed
- 1 cup mashed sweet potatoes
- ½ cup buttermilk

Instructions:

1. Preheat oven to 425°F.
2. Mix flour, baking powder, salt, and cinnamon.
3. Cut in butter, then stir in sweet potatoes and buttermilk.
4. Roll out and cut into biscuits.
5. Bake for 12-15 minutes.

Pumpkin Spice Biscuits

Ingredients:

- 2 cups all-purpose flour
- 1 tablespoon baking powder
- ½ teaspoon salt
- ½ teaspoon pumpkin spice
- ½ cup unsalted butter, cubed
- 1 cup pumpkin puree
- ½ cup buttermilk

Instructions:

1. Preheat oven to 425°F.
2. Mix flour, baking powder, salt, and pumpkin spice.
3. Cut in butter, then stir in pumpkin puree and buttermilk.
4. Roll out and cut into biscuits.
5. Bake for 12-15 minutes.

Jalapeño Cheddar Biscuits

Ingredients:

- 2 cups all-purpose flour
- 1 tablespoon baking powder
- ½ teaspoon salt
- ½ cup unsalted butter, cubed
- 1 cup shredded cheddar cheese
- 1 jalapeño, finely diced
- ¾ cup buttermilk

Instructions:

1. Preheat oven to 425°F.
2. Mix flour, baking powder, and salt.
3. Cut in butter, then stir in cheese, jalapeño, and buttermilk.
4. Roll out and cut into biscuits.
5. Bake for 12-15 minutes.

Blueberry Biscuits with Lemon Glaze

Ingredients:

- 2 cups all-purpose flour
- 1 tablespoon baking powder
- ½ teaspoon salt
- ½ cup cold butter, cubed
- 1 cup fresh blueberries
- ¾ cup buttermilk
- ½ cup powdered sugar
- 1 tablespoon lemon juice

Instructions:

1. Preheat oven to 425°F.
2. Mix flour, baking powder, and salt.
3. Cut in butter, then stir in blueberries and buttermilk.
4. Roll out and cut into biscuits.
5. Bake for 12-15 minutes.
6. Mix powdered sugar and lemon juice for glaze and drizzle over warm biscuits.

Whole Wheat Biscuits

Ingredients:

- 1 cup whole wheat flour
- 1 cup all-purpose flour
- 1 tablespoon baking powder
- ½ teaspoon salt
- ½ cup unsalted butter, cubed
- ¾ cup buttermilk

Instructions:

1. Preheat oven to 425°F.
2. Mix whole wheat flour, all-purpose flour, baking powder, and salt.
3. Cut in butter until mixture is crumbly.
4. Stir in buttermilk until just combined.
5. Roll out and cut into biscuits.
6. Bake for 12-15 minutes.

Cornmeal Biscuits

Ingredients:

- 1 cup all-purpose flour
- 1 cup cornmeal
- 1 tablespoon baking powder
- ½ teaspoon salt
- ½ cup cold butter, cubed
- ¾ cup buttermilk

Instructions:

1. Preheat oven to 425°F.
2. Combine flour, cornmeal, baking powder, and salt.
3. Cut in butter until crumbly.
4. Stir in buttermilk until dough comes together.
5. Roll out and cut into biscuits.
6. Bake for 12-15 minutes.

Cream Cheese Biscuits

Ingredients:

- 2 cups all-purpose flour
- 1 tablespoon baking powder
- ½ teaspoon salt
- ½ cup cold butter, cubed
- 4 ounces cream cheese, cubed
- ¾ cup buttermilk

Instructions:

1. Preheat oven to 425°F.
2. Mix flour, baking powder, and salt.
3. Cut in butter and cream cheese until mixture is crumbly.
4. Stir in buttermilk until combined.
5. Roll out and cut into biscuits.
6. Bake for 12-15 minutes.

Chocolate Chip Biscuits

Ingredients:

- 2 cups all-purpose flour
- 1 tablespoon baking powder
- ¼ cup sugar
- ½ teaspoon salt
- ½ cup cold butter, cubed
- ½ cup chocolate chips
- ¾ cup buttermilk

Instructions:

1. Preheat oven to 425°F.
2. Mix flour, baking powder, sugar, and salt.
3. Cut in butter until crumbly.
4. Stir in chocolate chips and buttermilk.
5. Roll out and cut into biscuits.
6. Bake for 12-15 minutes.

Maple Pecan Biscuits

Ingredients:

- 2 cups all-purpose flour
- 1 tablespoon baking powder
- ¼ teaspoon salt
- ½ cup unsalted butter, cubed
- ½ cup chopped pecans
- ¼ cup maple syrup
- ¾ cup buttermilk

Instructions:

1. Preheat oven to 425°F.
2. Mix flour, baking powder, and salt.
3. Cut in butter until crumbly.
4. Stir in pecans, maple syrup, and buttermilk.
5. Roll out and cut into biscuits.
6. Bake for 12-15 minutes.

Cinnamon Sugar Biscuits

Ingredients:

- 2 cups all-purpose flour
- 1 tablespoon baking powder
- ½ teaspoon salt
- ¼ cup sugar
- ½ teaspoon cinnamon
- ½ cup cold butter, cubed
- ¾ cup buttermilk

Instructions:

1. Preheat oven to 425°F.
2. Mix flour, baking powder, salt, sugar, and cinnamon.
3. Cut in butter until crumbly.
4. Stir in buttermilk until combined.
5. Roll out and cut into biscuits.
6. Bake for 12-15 minutes.

Herb and Parmesan Biscuits

Ingredients:

- 2 cups all-purpose flour
- 1 tablespoon baking powder
- ½ teaspoon salt
- ½ teaspoon dried rosemary
- ½ teaspoon dried thyme
- ½ cup grated Parmesan cheese
- ½ cup cold butter, cubed
- ¾ cup buttermilk

Instructions:

1. Preheat oven to 425°F.
2. Mix flour, baking powder, salt, rosemary, thyme, and Parmesan.
3. Cut in butter until crumbly.
4. Stir in buttermilk until combined.
5. Roll out and cut into biscuits.
6. Bake for 12-15 minutes.

Red Lobster-Style Biscuits

Ingredients:

- 2 cups all-purpose flour
- 1 tablespoon baking powder
- ½ teaspoon salt
- ½ teaspoon garlic powder
- ½ cup shredded cheddar cheese
- ½ cup cold butter, cubed
- ¾ cup buttermilk
- 2 tablespoons melted butter
- 1 tablespoon fresh parsley, chopped

Instructions:

1. Preheat oven to 450°F.
2. Mix flour, baking powder, salt, and garlic powder.
3. Cut in butter until crumbly, then stir in cheddar cheese and buttermilk.
4. Drop spoonfuls of dough onto a baking sheet.
5. Bake for 10-12 minutes.
6. Brush with melted butter and sprinkle with parsley.

Bacon and Cheddar Biscuits

Ingredients:

- 2 cups all-purpose flour
- 1 tablespoon baking powder
- ½ teaspoon salt
- ½ cup shredded cheddar cheese
- ½ cup cooked bacon, crumbled
- ½ cup cold butter, cubed
- ¾ cup buttermilk

Instructions:

1. Preheat oven to 425°F.
2. Mix flour, baking powder, and salt.
3. Cut in butter until crumbly.
4. Stir in cheddar cheese, bacon, and buttermilk.
5. Roll out and cut into biscuits.
6. Bake for 12-15 minutes.

Greek Yogurt Biscuits

Ingredients:

- 2 cups all-purpose flour
- 1 tablespoon baking powder
- ½ teaspoon salt
- ½ cup Greek yogurt
- ½ cup cold butter, cubed
- ½ cup milk

Instructions:

1. Preheat oven to 425°F.
2. Mix flour, baking powder, and salt.
3. Cut in butter until crumbly.
4. Stir in Greek yogurt and milk until combined.
5. Roll out and cut into biscuits.
6. Bake for 12-15 minutes.

Buttermilk Drop Biscuits

Ingredients:

- 2 cups all-purpose flour
- 1 tablespoon baking powder
- ½ teaspoon salt
- 1 teaspoon sugar
- ½ cup cold butter, cubed
- ¾ cup buttermilk

Instructions:

1. Preheat oven to 425°F.
2. Mix flour, baking powder, salt, and sugar.
3. Cut in butter until crumbly.
4. Stir in buttermilk until just combined.
5. Drop spoonfuls of dough onto a baking sheet.
6. Bake for 12-15 minutes.

Flaky Layered Biscuits

Ingredients:

- 2 cups all-purpose flour
- 1 tablespoon baking powder
- ½ teaspoon salt
- ½ cup cold butter, cubed
- ¾ cup buttermilk

Instructions:

1. Preheat oven to 425°F.
2. Mix flour, baking powder, and salt.
3. Cut in butter until crumbly.
4. Fold dough over itself several times for layers.
5. Roll out and cut into biscuits.
6. Bake for 12-15 minutes.

Cranberry Orange Biscuits

Ingredients:

- 2 cups all-purpose flour
- 1 tablespoon baking powder
- ½ teaspoon salt
- ¼ cup sugar
- ½ cup dried cranberries
- Zest of 1 orange
- ½ cup cold butter, cubed
- ¾ cup buttermilk

Instructions:

1. Preheat oven to 425°F.
2. Mix flour, baking powder, salt, sugar, cranberries, and orange zest.
3. Cut in butter until crumbly.
4. Stir in buttermilk until combined.
5. Roll out and cut into biscuits.
6. Bake for 12-15 minutes.

Almond Flour Biscuits (Gluten-Free)

Ingredients:

- 2 cups almond flour
- 1 teaspoon baking powder
- ½ teaspoon salt
- 2 tablespoons butter, melted
- 2 eggs
- ¼ cup heavy cream

Instructions:

1. Preheat oven to 350°F.
2. Mix almond flour, baking powder, and salt.
3. Stir in butter, eggs, and heavy cream.
4. Drop spoonfuls onto a baking sheet.
5. Bake for 15-18 minutes.

Sourdough Biscuits

Ingredients:

- 2 cups all-purpose flour
- 1 tablespoon baking powder
- ½ teaspoon salt
- ½ cup cold butter, cubed
- 1 cup sourdough starter

Instructions:

1. Preheat oven to 425°F.
2. Mix flour, baking powder, and salt.
3. Cut in butter until crumbly.
4. Stir in sourdough starter until combined.
5. Roll out and cut into biscuits.
6. Bake for 12-15 minutes.

Classic French Baguette

Ingredients:

- 3 ½ cups bread flour
- 1 ½ teaspoons salt
- 1 teaspoon sugar
- 2 teaspoons yeast
- 1 ¼ cups warm water

Instructions:

1. Mix flour, salt, sugar, and yeast.
2. Add warm water and knead until smooth.
3. Let rise for 1 hour.
4. Shape into baguettes and let rise for another 30 minutes.
5. Bake at 450°F for 20-25 minutes.

Sourdough Bread

Ingredients:

- 4 cups bread flour
- 1 ½ teaspoons salt
- 1 cup sourdough starter
- 1 ½ cups warm water

Instructions:

1. Mix flour and salt.
2. Add sourdough starter and water, mix well.
3. Let rise for 4-6 hours.
4. Shape into a loaf and let rise for 1 more hour.
5. Bake at 450°F for 30-35 minutes.

Ciabatta Bread

Ingredients:

- 3 ½ cups bread flour
- 1 teaspoon salt
- 1 teaspoon sugar
- 2 teaspoons yeast
- 1 ½ cups warm water

Instructions:

1. Mix flour, salt, sugar, and yeast.
2. Add warm water and knead until sticky.
3. Let rise for 2 hours.
4. Shape into loaves and let rise for another 30 minutes.
5. Bake at 425°F for 25-30 minutes.

Focaccia with Rosemary and Sea Salt

Ingredients:

- 4 cups all-purpose flour
- 2 teaspoons salt
- 2 teaspoons yeast
- 1 ½ cups warm water
- ¼ cup olive oil
- 2 tablespoons fresh rosemary
- 1 teaspoon sea salt

Instructions:

1. Mix flour, salt, yeast, and warm water.
2. Knead until smooth and let rise for 1 hour.
3. Press into a baking pan and drizzle with olive oil.
4. Sprinkle rosemary and sea salt on top.
5. Bake at 425°F for 20-25 minutes.

Brioche Loaf

Ingredients:

- 3 ½ cups bread flour
- ¼ cup sugar
- 1 ½ teaspoons salt
- 2 teaspoons yeast
- 3 eggs
- ½ cup warm milk
- ½ cup unsalted butter, softened

Instructions:

1. Mix flour, sugar, salt, and yeast.
2. Add eggs and warm milk, mix well.
3. Knead in butter until smooth.
4. Let rise for 2 hours.
5. Shape into a loaf and let rise for 1 more hour.
6. Bake at 375°F for 30-35 minutes.

Challah Bread

Ingredients:

- 4 cups all-purpose flour
- 2 ¼ teaspoons yeast
- ¼ cup sugar
- 1 teaspoon salt
- ⅓ cup vegetable oil
- 2 eggs + 1 for egg wash
- ¾ cup warm water

Instructions:

1. In a bowl, mix yeast, warm water, and sugar. Let sit for 10 minutes.
2. Add oil, eggs, salt, and flour. Knead until smooth.
3. Let rise for 1 ½ hours.
4. Braid dough and let rise for another 30 minutes.
5. Brush with egg wash and bake at 375°F for 25-30 minutes.

Garlic Knots

Ingredients:

- 2 ½ cups all-purpose flour
- 2 teaspoons yeast
- 1 teaspoon salt
- ¾ cup warm water
- 2 tablespoons olive oil
- 3 tablespoons melted butter
- 3 cloves garlic, minced
- 1 tablespoon parsley

Instructions:

1. Mix flour, yeast, salt, warm water, and olive oil. Knead until smooth.
2. Let rise for 1 hour.
3. Divide dough, roll into strips, and tie into knots. Let rise for 30 minutes.
4. Bake at 375°F for 15 minutes.
5. Brush with melted butter, garlic, and parsley.

Italian Herb and Cheese Bread

Ingredients:

- 3 ½ cups bread flour
- 2 teaspoons yeast
- 1 teaspoon salt
- 1 teaspoon Italian seasoning
- ½ cup shredded Parmesan
- 1 cup warm water
- 2 tablespoons olive oil

Instructions:

1. Mix flour, yeast, salt, and Italian seasoning.
2. Add warm water and olive oil. Knead until smooth.
3. Let rise for 1 hour.
4. Shape into a loaf and let rise for 30 minutes.
5. Sprinkle Parmesan on top and bake at 375°F for 25-30 minutes.

Pita Bread

Ingredients:

- 3 cups all-purpose flour
- 2 teaspoons yeast
- 1 teaspoon salt
- 1 teaspoon sugar
- 1 cup warm water
- 1 tablespoon olive oil

Instructions:

1. Mix flour, yeast, salt, sugar, water, and olive oil. Knead until smooth.
2. Let rise for 1 hour.
3. Divide into small rounds and roll into ¼-inch thick circles.
4. Bake at 475°F for 5-7 minutes.

Naan Bread

Ingredients:

- 2 ½ cups all-purpose flour
- 2 teaspoons yeast
- ½ teaspoon salt
- 1 teaspoon sugar
- ¾ cup warm milk
- ¼ cup plain yogurt
- 2 tablespoons melted butter

Instructions:

1. Mix flour, yeast, salt, sugar, milk, and yogurt. Knead until smooth.
2. Let rise for 1 hour.
3. Divide into pieces and roll into flat rounds.
4. Cook on a hot skillet for 1-2 minutes per side.
5. Brush with melted butter.

Cornbread Muffins

Ingredients:

- 1 cup cornmeal
- 1 cup all-purpose flour
- 1 tablespoon baking powder
- ½ teaspoon salt
- ¼ cup sugar
- 1 cup buttermilk
- 1 egg
- ¼ cup melted butter

Instructions:

1. Preheat oven to 375°F.
2. Mix cornmeal, flour, baking powder, salt, and sugar.
3. Add buttermilk, egg, and melted butter. Stir until combined.
4. Pour into muffin tins and bake for 15-18 minutes.

Honey Oat Bread

Ingredients:

- 3 cups bread flour
- 1 cup rolled oats
- 2 teaspoons yeast
- 1 teaspoon salt
- ¼ cup honey
- 1 cup warm water
- 2 tablespoons butter

Instructions:

1. Mix flour, oats, yeast, and salt.
2. Add honey, water, and butter. Knead until smooth.
3. Let rise for 1 hour.
4. Shape into a loaf and let rise for 30 minutes.
5. Bake at 375°F for 25-30 minutes.

Rye Bread

Ingredients:

- 2 cups rye flour
- 2 cups bread flour
- 2 teaspoons yeast
- 1 teaspoon salt
- 1 tablespoon sugar
- 1 cup warm water
- 2 tablespoons olive oil

Instructions:

1. Mix rye flour, bread flour, yeast, salt, and sugar.
2. Add warm water and olive oil. Knead until smooth.
3. Let rise for 1 hour.
4. Shape into a loaf and let rise for 30 minutes.
5. Bake at 375°F for 30-35 minutes.

French Toast Bread

Ingredients:

- 4 cups all-purpose flour
- 2 teaspoons yeast
- 1 teaspoon salt
- ¼ cup sugar
- 1 teaspoon cinnamon
- ¾ cup warm milk
- 2 eggs
- ¼ cup melted butter

Instructions:

1. Mix flour, yeast, salt, sugar, and cinnamon.
2. Add warm milk, eggs, and melted butter. Knead until smooth.
3. Let rise for 1 hour.
4. Shape into a loaf and let rise for 30 minutes.
5. Bake at 375°F for 25-30 minutes.

Cinnamon Swirl Bread

Ingredients:

- 4 cups all-purpose flour
- 2 teaspoons yeast
- 1 teaspoon salt
- ¼ cup sugar
- ¾ cup warm milk
- 1 egg
- ¼ cup melted butter
- ¼ cup brown sugar
- 1 teaspoon cinnamon

Instructions:

1. Mix flour, yeast, salt, sugar, warm milk, egg, and butter. Knead until smooth.
2. Let rise for 1 hour.
3. Roll out dough, spread with brown sugar and cinnamon.
4. Roll into a loaf shape and let rise for 30 minutes.
5. Bake at 375°F for 25-30 minutes.

Banana Bread

Ingredients:

- 2 cups all-purpose flour
- 1 teaspoon baking soda
- ½ teaspoon salt
- ½ cup butter, melted
- ¾ cup brown sugar
- 2 eggs
- 3 ripe bananas, mashed
- 1 teaspoon vanilla extract

Instructions:

1. Preheat oven to 350°F (175°C). Grease a loaf pan.
2. In a bowl, mix flour, baking soda, and salt.
3. In another bowl, mix melted butter, sugar, eggs, bananas, and vanilla.
4. Combine wet and dry ingredients, stirring until just mixed.
5. Pour into loaf pan and bake for 50-60 minutes.

Zucchini Bread

Ingredients:

- 2 cups all-purpose flour
- 1 teaspoon baking soda
- ½ teaspoon baking powder
- ½ teaspoon salt
- 1 teaspoon cinnamon
- ½ cup vegetable oil
- ¾ cup sugar
- 2 eggs
- 1 teaspoon vanilla extract
- 1 ½ cups grated zucchini

Instructions:

1. Preheat oven to 350°F (175°C). Grease a loaf pan.
2. Mix flour, baking soda, baking powder, salt, and cinnamon.
3. In another bowl, mix oil, sugar, eggs, and vanilla.
4. Combine wet and dry ingredients, then fold in zucchini.
5. Pour into loaf pan and bake for 50-55 minutes.

Pumpkin Bread

Ingredients:

- 1 ¾ cups all-purpose flour
- 1 teaspoon baking soda
- ½ teaspoon salt
- 1 teaspoon cinnamon
- ½ teaspoon nutmeg
- ½ cup vegetable oil
- ¾ cup sugar
- 2 eggs
- 1 cup pumpkin puree
- 1 teaspoon vanilla extract

Instructions:

1. Preheat oven to 350°F (175°C). Grease a loaf pan.
2. Mix flour, baking soda, salt, cinnamon, and nutmeg.
3. In another bowl, mix oil, sugar, eggs, pumpkin, and vanilla.
4. Combine wet and dry ingredients and mix until smooth.
5. Pour into loaf pan and bake for 50-55 minutes.

Cranberry Walnut Bread

Ingredients:

- 2 cups all-purpose flour
- 1 teaspoon baking soda
- ½ teaspoon salt
- ½ teaspoon cinnamon
- ¾ cup sugar
- ½ cup orange juice
- ¼ cup melted butter
- 1 egg
- 1 cup fresh cranberries, chopped
- ½ cup walnuts, chopped

Instructions:

1. Preheat oven to 350°F (175°C). Grease a loaf pan.
2. Mix flour, baking soda, salt, cinnamon, and sugar.
3. In another bowl, mix orange juice, butter, and egg.
4. Combine wet and dry ingredients, then fold in cranberries and walnuts.
5. Pour into loaf pan and bake for 50-55 minutes.

Cheddar Jalapeño Bread

Ingredients:

- 3 cups all-purpose flour
- 1 tablespoon baking powder
- ½ teaspoon salt
- 1 cup shredded cheddar cheese
- 1 jalapeño, finely chopped
- 1 cup buttermilk
- 2 eggs
- ¼ cup melted butter

Instructions:

1. Preheat oven to 350°F (175°C). Grease a loaf pan.
2. Mix flour, baking powder, salt, cheese, and jalapeño.
3. In another bowl, mix buttermilk, eggs, and melted butter.
4. Combine wet and dry ingredients.
5. Pour into loaf pan and bake for 50-55 minutes.

Pretzel Bread Rolls

Ingredients:

- 3 ½ cups all-purpose flour
- 1 packet (2 ¼ tsp) yeast
- 1 teaspoon salt
- 1 cup warm water
- 2 tablespoons butter, melted
- ¼ cup baking soda (for boiling water)
- 1 egg, beaten (for brushing)

Instructions:

1. Mix flour, yeast, and salt. Add warm water and melted butter. Knead until smooth.
2. Let rise for 1 hour.
3. Divide into small rolls.
4. Bring a pot of water to a boil, add baking soda, and dip each roll for 30 seconds.
5. Place on a baking sheet, brush with egg wash, and bake at 400°F for 15-20 minutes.

Olive and Herb Focaccia

Ingredients:

- 3 ½ cups all-purpose flour
- 1 packet (2 ¼ tsp) yeast
- 1 teaspoon salt
- 1 teaspoon Italian herbs
- 1 ¼ cups warm water
- ¼ cup olive oil
- ½ cup black olives, sliced

Instructions:

1. Mix flour, yeast, salt, and herbs. Add warm water and olive oil. Knead until smooth.
2. Let rise for 1 hour.
3. Spread dough onto a greased baking sheet. Press olives into the dough.
4. Let rise for 30 minutes.
5. Drizzle with olive oil and bake at 400°F for 20-25 minutes.

Potato Bread

Ingredients:

- 3 cups all-purpose flour
- 1 cup mashed potatoes
- 1 packet (2 ¼ tsp) yeast
- 1 teaspoon salt
- 1 teaspoon sugar
- ¾ cup warm water
- 2 tablespoons butter, melted

Instructions:

1. Mix flour, mashed potatoes, yeast, salt, and sugar.
2. Add warm water and melted butter. Knead until smooth.
3. Let rise for 1 hour.
4. Shape into a loaf and let rise for 30 minutes.
5. Bake at 375°F for 30-35 minutes.

Multigrain Seeded Bread

Ingredients:

- 2 cups whole wheat flour
- 1 cup all-purpose flour
- ¼ cup sunflower seeds
- ¼ cup flaxseeds
- 1 packet (2 ¼ tsp) yeast
- 1 teaspoon salt
- 1 cup warm water

- 2 tablespoons honey

Instructions:

1. Mix flours, seeds, yeast, and salt.
2. Add warm water and honey. Knead until smooth.
3. Let rise for 1 hour.
4. Shape into a loaf and let rise for 30 minutes.
5. Bake at 375°F for 30-35 minutes.

Beer Bread

Ingredients:

- 3 cups self-rising flour
- ¼ cup sugar
- 1 bottle (12 oz) beer
- 2 tablespoons melted butter

Instructions:

1. Preheat oven to 375°F (190°C). Grease a loaf pan.
2. Mix flour, sugar, and beer. Stir until combined.
3. Pour into loaf pan and drizzle with melted butter.
4. Bake for 45-50 minutes.